AVENGERS
THE INITIATIVE

KILLED IN ACTION

WRITERS: DAN SLOTT & CHRISTOS N. GAGE
ARTIST: STEFANO CASELLI
WITH STEVE UY (ISSUE #12-13)
COLOR ART: DANIELE RUDONI WITH STEVE UY (ISSUE #12-13)
COVER ART: STEFANO CASELLI & STEVE UY

ANNUAL #1

WRITERS: DAN SLOTT WITH CHRISTOS N. GAGE
ARTISTS: SALVADOR LARROCA, CLAYTON HENRY
& PAUL NEARY, STEVE UY, TOM FEISTER
& CARMINE DI GIANDOMENICO AND
PATRICK SCHERBERGER & DAVE MEIKIS
COLOR ART: STEPHANE PERU, DANIELE RUDONI, STEVE UY,
JOSE VILLARRUBIA & WIL QUINTANA
COVER ART: JIM CHEUNG

LETTERER: VIRTUAL CALLIGRAPHY'S JOE CARAMAGNA
ASSISTANT EDITOR: MOLLY LAZER
EDITOR: TOM BREVOORT

COLLECTION EDITOR: JENNIFER GRÜNWALD
ASSISTANT EDITORS: CORY LEVINE & JOHN DENNING
EDITOR, SPECIAL PROJECTS: MARK D. BEAZLEY
SENIOR EDITOR, SPECIAL PROJECTS: JEFF YOUNGQUIST
SENIOR VICE PRESIDENT OF SALES: DAVID GABRIEL
PRODUCTION: NELSON RIBEIRO
VICE PRESIDENT OF CREATIVE: TOM MARVELLI

EDITOR IN CHIEF: JOE QUESADA
PUBLISHER: DAN BUCKLEY

AVENGERS: THE INITIATIVE VOL. 2 — KILLED IN ACTION. Contains material originally published in magazine form as AVENGERS: THE INITIATIVE #7-13 and ANNUAL #1. First printing 2008. Hardcover ISBN# 978-0-7851-2868-7. Softcover ISBN# 978-0-7851-2861-8. Published by MARVEL PUBLISHING, INC., a subsidiary of MARVEL ENTERTAINMENT, INC. OFFICE OF PUBLICATION: 417 5th Avenue, New York, NY 10016. Copyright © 2007 and 2008 Marvel Characters, Inc. All rights reserved. Hardcover: $24.99 per copy in the U.S. and $26.50 in Canada (GST #R127032852). Softcover: $19.99 per copy in the U.S. and $21.00 in Canada (GST #R127032852). Canadian Agreement #40668537. All characters featured in this issue and the distinctive names and likenesses thereof, and all related indicia are trademarks of Marvel Characters, Inc. No similarity between any of the names, characters, persons, and/or institutions in this magazine with those of any living or dead person or institution is intended, and any such similarity which may exist is purely coincidental. **Printed in the U.S.A.** ALAN FINE, CEO Marvel Toys & Publishing Divisions and CMO Marvel Entertainment, Inc.; DAVID GABRIEL, SVP of Publishing Sales & Circulation; DAVID BOGART, SVP of Business Affairs & Talent Management; MICHAEL PASCIULLO, VP of Merchandising & Communications; JIM O'KEEFE, VP of Operations & Logistics; DAN CARR, Executive Director of Publishing Technology; JUSTIN F. GABRIE, Director of Editorial Operations; SUSAN CRESPI, Editorial Operations Manager; OMAR OTIEKU, Production Manager; STAN LEE, Chairman Emeritus. For information regarding advertising in Marvel Comics or on Marvel.com, please contact Mitch Dane, Advertising Director, at mdane@marvel.com. For Marvel subscription inquiries, please call 800-217-9158.

10 9 8 7 6 5 4 3 2 1

AVENGERS
THE INITIATIVE

After Stamford, Connecticut was destroyed during a televised fight between the New Warriors and a group of dangerous villains, a federal superhuman registration act was passed. All individuals possessing paranormal abilities must now register with the government. Tony Stark, a.k.a. Iron Man, has been appointed director of S.H.I.E.L.D., the international peacekeeping force. He has set in motion the Initiative, a plan for training and policing super heroes in this brave new world, intended to position a local super hero team in each of America's fifty states.

STAFF

| YELLOW JACKET | JUSTICE | THE GAUNTLET | WAR MACHINE | BARON VON BLITZSCHLAG | HENRY PETER GYRICH |

TRAINEES

| SCARLET SPIDERS | CLOUD 9 | MVP (DECEASED?) |

CIVILIANS

| PETER PARKER/SPIDER-MAN | J. JONAH JAMESON | BETTY BRANT |

When a training exercise goes awry, MVP — the most promising trainee in the Initiative — is killed. All those present in the room during the accident are told the incident never happened. However, on a visit to MVP's home in Kentucky, Justice and Cloud 9 discover Michael Van Patrick, very much alive!

When the Hulk threatened New York City and a group of Initiative members were captured, Gyrich sent in the Shadow Initiative, a black ops team that included the three mysterious Scarlet Spiders, to rescue them. Hulk destroyed much of Manhattan — including Stark Tower, headquarters of the Avengers — but the Initiative trainees came out relatively unharmed.

Meanwhile, apart from the destruction wrought by the Hulk, May Parker, aunt of Peter Parker (a.k.a. Spider-Man), lies in a Manhattan hospital on life support after being shot by a sniper.

#7

WHAT'S THE SITUATION HERE, GYRICH?

THE SCARLET SPIDERS, OUR PREMIER STEALTH UNIT...

...HANDPICKED MEMBERS OF MY SPECIAL FORCES TEAM...

...HAVE JUST *OUTED* *THEMSELVES* TO THE GENERAL PUBLIC.

YOUR SPECIAL FORCES TEAM?

YOU PEOPLE REALIZE THIS IS MY BASE, RIGHT?

YOU KEEP THINKING THAT, RHODES. WHAT *I* WANT TO KNOW...

...IS WHAT THEY WERE DOING *OFF* BASE WITHOUT *MY* PERMISSION?!

THEY ACCOMPANIED THE BARON TO THE GAMMA DEFENSE SUMMIT.

IT SEEMS THEY'VE GROWN...QUITE ATTACHED TO HIM.

WAIT. WHY HAVE THE SPIDERS ACTIVATED THEMSELVES?

WHAT COULD BE SO IMPORTANT THAT THEY'D COMPROMISE THEIR--

SUPER-VILLAINS.

BUNCH OF THIRD-RATERS, THE VULTURIONS, STOLE SOME OF OUR TOP-SECRET PLANS FOR GAMMA RAY TECHNOLOGY. THE SPIDERS ARE IN PURSUIT.

WHAT?! LIKE PLANS TO MAKE GAMMA BOMBS?!

DON'T BE SUCH A DRAMA QUEEN, RHODES. OUR BEST AND BRIGHTEST ARE ON IT. AND EACH ONE OF 'EM HAS SPIDER-POWERS.

THAT'S *MY* LIKENESS, PAL! BUT DON'T WORRY, WHEN I'M DONE...

...ALL YOU'RE GONNA RESEMBLE IS A *BIG, RED SMEAR!*

COMMANDER, COME IN! WE HAVE A PROBLEM!

PETER PARKER HAS ENTERED THE FIELD OF ENGAGEMENT.

HE'S TARGETED RED TEAM ONE. SHOULD WE BREAK PURSUIT?

PARKER?

NEGATIVE! STAY ON THE LEAD VULTURION. HE CAN'T GET AWAY WITH THOSE PLANS!

BUT SIR--

THAT'S AN ORDER!

COPY THAT.

RED TEAM THREE! STAY IN FORMATION!

NO CAN-DO, SIR. I WON'T LEAVE A MAN BEHIND!

WELL, THAT CERTAINLY CHANGES THINGS.

THREE AGAINST ONE? LET'S DO IT!

RED TEAM THREE, COPY?

PAT? I NEED SOME BACKUP! DON'T LEAVE ME HANGIN' HERE!

"ARE YOU GETTING THIS?"

TELL ME YOU'RE GETTING THIS! THE STUDIO SAYS THEY'RE READY TO CUT TO US LIVE!

HEY, WE'RE GOOD TO GO.

THIS IS GREG FOREST, ON THE UPPER WEST SIDE...

"...COMING TO YOU LIVE, WITH A SUPERHUMAN BRAWL IN PROGRESS...

The S.H.I.E.L.D. Helicarrier.

"...BETWEEN WHAT APPEAR TO BE TWO SPIDER-MEN...

Times Square.

"...AND AN UNIDENTIFIED ASSAILANT-- WAIT!"

"WE'RE GOING IN CLOSER. YES, WE CAN NOW CONFIRM..."

"...THE THIRD MAN IS NONE OTHER THAN THE FUGITIVE KNOWN AS--"

PARKER?!!

PETER PARKER? WHAT IN BLAZES IS GOING ON HERE?!

GEEZ, MR. JAMESON, HOW MANY SPIDER-MEN DO YOU THINK THERE ARE?

WELL, THIS BETTER NOT

The Daily

GOD, I HATE CLONES.

LET ME GUESS, YOU'RE PART OF THE INITIATIVE, RIGHT? SO WHATCHA SUPPOSED TO BE? TONY STARK'S SPIDER SLAYERS?

SC-SCARLET SPIDERS...

REAL ORIGINAL.

STOP IT, PARKER! WHAT'S MORE IMPORTANT HERE? LASHING OUT AT STARK'S INITIATIVE?

OR DOING WHAT'S RIGHT? WHAT HAPPENED TO THE MAN WHO SAID THIS:

(PLAY AUDIO FILE: PARKER 21:03)

"THE BAD GUYS ARE GETTING AWAY!

AW, MAN. WAY TO THROW THAT BACK IN MY FACE.

BUT YOU'RE RIGHT...

"BUT NO! YOU'D RATHER PLAY 'TAKE SHOTS AT SPIDEY.' PRIORITIES, PEOPLE!"*

*SPIDEY SAYS THIS IN A:TI #3. —TOM.

"...I'M NOT BEING RESPONSIBLE."

AGAIN! THERE'S STILL SOME LIFE LEFT IN 'IM!

NOT FOR MUCH LONGER!

FWUNK!

ONE SIDE, KIDS. BETTER LET DADDY TAKE THIS ONE.

THESE GUYS DON'T SEEM TOO IMPRESSED WITH THIS YEAR'S MODELS.

HE HAS A POINT.

WELL, THESE SUITS DO HAVE A FEATURE WE HAVEN'T USED YET.

YOU READ MY MIND.

BUT FOR THE RECORD, THAT WON'T BE ME. FOR THE RECORD.

AND THERE YOU HAVE IT, AN ACTION 8 EXCLUSIVE...

WAIT! SO IS HE OR *ISN'T* HE?

OH, HE *TOTALLY* IS. ORRR MAYBE NOT...

IS PETER PARKER THE SPECTACULAR SPIDER-MAN? NEW DOUBTS HAVE BEEN CAST HERE TODAY.

ALONG WITH THE STARTLING DISCOVERY THAT *THREE MORE* SPIDER-MEN ARE OUT THERE...

"...THREE SPIDER-MEN WITH ALLEGED TIES TO THE U.S. GOVERNMENT--"

TURN THAT #$&@#%$ THING *OFF!*

COM SYSTEM: OVERRIDE. RED TEAM, SOUND OFF!

RED TEAM HERE, COMMANDER.

STATUS?

CAPE-KILLERS HAVE THE VULTURIONS IN CUSTODY. AND THE CASE IS SECURE.

IS THE BARON...?

HE'S FINE. NOW, SUIT UP.

YOU ALL HAVE A HELL OF A LOT OF EXPLAINING TO DO WHEN YOU

ANNUAL #1

FIFTY STATE INITIATIVE

Dan Slott with Christos Gage - Writers

"SECOND BEST"
Salvador Larroca - Artist
Stephane Peru - Color Art

"REASON FOR BEING"
Clayton Henry - Penciler
Paul Neary - Inker
Daniele Rudoni - Colorist

"BE ALL THAT YOU CAN BE"
Steve Uy - Artist

"BORN TO SERVE"
Tom Feister & Carmine Di Giandomenico - Artists
Jose Villarrubia - Color Art

"STATE OF READINESS"
Patrick Scherberger - Penciler
David Meikis - Inker
Wil Quintana - Colorist

VC's Joe Caramagna - Letterer

Molly Lazer - Assistant Editor
Tom Brevoort - Editor
Joe Quesada - Editor in Chief
Dan Buckley - Publisher

THE LIBERTEENS

GAUNTLET
SGT. JOSEPH GREEN

ARMORY
VIOLET LIGHTNER

MVP
MICHAEL VAN PATRICK

HARDBALL
ROGER BROKERIDGE

WHERE THEY CAME FROM.

"JUST THAT TWO ENERGY SOURCES OF INCALCULABLE POWER SUDDENLY APPEARED ABOVE OUR PLANET...

"...COLLIDED WITH ONE ANOTHER...

"...AND BROKE APART.

"AS THEY FELL INTO THE ATMOSPHERE, THE FRAGMENTS WERE THROWN IN MULTIPLE DIRECTIONS, TOWARD DIFFERENT PARTS OF THE GLOBE.

"OUR SATELLITES TRACKED THEM AS BEST THEY COULD...

THE GAUNTLET IN "SECOND BEST"

The End

"I DIDN'T KNOW WHAT IT WAS, THIS... *THING* WRAPPING ITSELF AROUND MY ARM.

"BUT *IT* KNEW.

"IT'S NOT LIKE IT SPOKE TO ME OR ANYTHING. BUT SOMEHOW I *UNDERSTOOD* WHAT IT WAS. A *WEAPON*, FROM... SOMEWHERE ELSE...

"AND IT KNEW WHAT *I* NEEDED.

"...THAT COULD BECOME WHATEVER ITS WEARER NEEDED THE MOST. AND WHAT I NEEDED MOST IN MY *PERSONAL* BATTLE...

"...WAS A REASON FOR BEING.

I REMEMBER THE AVENGERS FIGHTING THAT ROBOT, BUT NO MENTION OF YOU. WHAT HAPPENED NEXT?

WELL, THAT'S THE KICKER, DOC. I CAN'T REALLY *TELL* YOU.

THEY SENT ME TO *CAMP HAMMOND,* THE BOOT CAMP FOR HEROES IN TRAINING. ALONG WITH OTHERS LIKE *TRAUMA, KOMODO, CLOUD NINE* AND *HARDBALL.*

BUT EVERYTHING THAT HAPPENS THERE IS *CLASSIFIED.*

YOU WERE DOING GREAT, AND THEN? DID SOMETHING GO WRONG?

HEH. TRY *EVERYTHING.*

TRAUMA, WHOSE POWER IS TO BECOME WHATEVER SCARES YOU MOST, TURNED INTO A *GIANT SPIDER.*

VIOLET, YOU HAVE TO OPEN UP. YOU CAN TELL ME ANYTHING. IT'S ALL *CONFIDENTIAL;* NO ONE ELSE WILL EVER KNOW.

WHATEVER HAPPENED-- WHATEVER YOU MIGHT HAVE *DONE*-- WE CAN WORK *THROUGH* IT.

The End

CONGRESSMAN. GOT SOME NEW CRYSTALS IN THAT CAN HELP ADJUST YOUR CHAKRAS.

IT'S ME, IDIOT, AND I'M LATE. JUST OPEN IT.

DON'T KNOW WHAT YOU'RE TALKING ABOUT, SIR.

SIGH. TODAY'S PASSWORD IS "DRESDEN."

HAVE A NICE DAY, MR. WOODMAN.

VVVMM

HAIL HYDRA! IMMORTAL HYDRA! CUT OFF A LIMB AND TWO MORE SHALL TAKE ITS PLACE!

COMMANDER WOODMAN, HYDRA COMMANDERS FROM THROUGHOUT THE COUNTRY HAVE COME TO HEAR YOUR REPORT.

TELL US ALL WE NEED TO KNOW ABOUT HARDBALL.

THE BOY'S CIVILIAN NAME IS *ROGER BROKERIDGE*. HE GREW UP IN A SUBURB OF LOS ANGELES...

"...IN A BOURGEOIS MIDDLE-CLASS FAMILY THAT WAS RECENTLY FACED WITH THE HARSH *REALITY* UNDERLYING THEIR PRECIOUS 'AMERICAN DREAM.'"

MR. BROKERIDGE. MRS. BROKERIDGE. I'M AFRAID THE NEWS ISN'T GOOD.

PAUL'S CONDITION IS WORSENING AND THERE'S VERY LITTLE I CAN DO...YOUR SON HAS NEEDS A SMALL-TOWN DOCTOR JUST CAN'T MEET.

YOU'VE SEEN HIM; HE CAN'T BE MOVED. AND WE CAN'T AFFORD TO BRING IN SPECIALISTS ANYMORE.

I'M SORRY. I WISH I HAD AN ANSWER FOR YOU...BUT I'M NOT SURE THERE IS ONE.

CH-CHK

RUH... ROGER?

I'M GONNA DO IT, PAUL. THIS TIME I'M GONNA...I...

AW, HELL, PAUL...I'M NOT SURE I CAN.

'S OKAY, BRO. BULLET... PROLLY WOULDN' WORK...ANYHOW.

'M SORRY, ROG. SO... SORRY.

WHAT WERE YOU *THINKING*, PAUL? BEING A REGULAR WRESTLER ON STEROIDS WASN'T BAD ENOUGH? YOU HAD TO JOIN THAT LEAGUE FOR *SUPER-FREAKS?*

I SWEAR, IF I EVER FOUND THAT GUY WHO GAVE YOU YOUR POWERS, I'D--

KRESH

THE POWER BROKER...

ROG, NO! C'M BACK!

ROGER!!

YOU WERE WISE TO COME SEE ME, ROGER. JUST BY LOOKING AT YOU, I CAN TELL YOU'RE A YOUNG MAN WITH BIG DREAMS.

I'M THE KIND OF PERSON THAT CAN MAKE THOSE DREAMS COME TRUE.

BUT BE WARNED... TRUE POWER ALWAYS COMES WITH A PRICE.

ARE YOU PREPARED TO PAY THAT PRICE, ROGER?

THE ONLY ONE WHO'S GONNA PAY IS YOU!

DID YOU USE THAT LAME SALES PITCH ON MY BROTHER? TELL HIM HE'D BE THE UNLIMITED CLASS WRESTLING FEDERATION CHAMP?

YOU MADE HIM THINK HE WAS UNBEATABLE! YOU NEVER TOLD HIM YOU'D MAKE OTHER GUYS EVEN STRONGER THAN HIM!

ONE BAD MATCH AND NOW HE'S CRIPPLED FOR LIFE! MY FAMILY'S GONNA LOSE EVERYTHING! WELL, GUESS WHAT, BIG SHOT--SO ARE YOU!

HEH. WRONG.

ZZZKKT

WHAT? YOU THINK WHEN I BECAME THE NEW POWER BROKER, I'D GIVE POWERS TO OTHERS AND *NOT* MYSELF?

DON'T BE SO NAÏVE, ROGER. I HAVE *MORE* POWER THAN YOU COULD EVER IMAGINE.

WHAT YOU DON'T REALIZE IS THAT *YOU* DO, TOO.

YOU HAVE THE GREATEST POWER OF ALL, ROGER-- *DESPERATION.* WHEN SOMEONE HAS NOTHING LEFT TO LOSE...THEY'RE CAPABLE OF *ANYTHING.*

IMAGINE SOMEONE LIKE THAT BEING GIVEN *TRUE* POWER. WHO KNOWS WHAT THEY COULD ACCOMPLISH?

HAH! NO, ROGER. SOMETHING FAR MORE USEFUL THAN THAT.

SEVENTY PERCENT. WHATEVER FEES YOU'RE PAID, WHATEVER GOODS YOU STEAL, WHATEVER CONS YOU PULL... I GET SEVENTY PERCENT.

SO...DO WE HAVE A DEAL?

I COULD GIVE YOU THAT POWER. ENOUGH TO GET YOUR FAMILY ALL THE MONEY THEY'D EVER NEED. TO GIVE YOU THE LIFE YOU'VE ALWAYS WANTED.

BUT AS I SAID...IT COMES WITH A *PRICE.*

MY...MY *SOUL?*

"I WON'T LIE TO YOU, ROGER. IT'S GOING TO HURT. A LOT."

"BUT THE PAIN WILL FADE... AND THE *POWER* WILL REMAIN."

OKAY... FIRST TIME FOR EVERYTHING. IT'S NATURAL TO BE NERVOUS. BUT YOU'VE BEEN CASING THIS ROUTE FOR WEEKS.

NOTHING TO BE SCARED OF. YOU'RE READY. IT'S THE *WORLD* THAT ISN'T READY...

...FOR *HARDBALL!*

OH YEAH... WHAT A RUSH! WITH THIS POWER, AN ARMORED CAR'S LIKE A TIN CAN TO--

HUH?

WHA-KOOM

UH...YOU OKAY, KID?

HEY, NICE GOIN', PAL! NO WAY I COULDA STOPPED IN TIME.

SUSIE! OH, THANK THE LORD...

...AND THANK YOU, SIR. I DON'T KNOW WHO YOU ARE, BUT YOU'RE A HERO.

I CONCUR, FRIEND. AND I OWE YOU ONE, FOR STEPPING IN WHEN I WAS TOO FAR AWAY.

ARE YOU CLAIRVOYANT, TOO? OR IS IT JUST THE ENERGY POWERS?

UH, JUST THE ENERGY, MR. WONDER MAN, SIR.

CALL ME SIMON. THEN HOW DID YOU KNOW--?

I'M HARDBALL. AND I GUESS I WAS IN THE RIGHT PLACE AT THE RIGHT TIME.

IN MORE WAYS THAN ONE. TELL ME, HARDBALL, ARE YOU FAMILIAR WITH THE INITIATIVE?

AND THE FOOLS **REGISTERED** HIM. JUST LIKE THAT. LITTLE KNOWING HIS TRUE SECRET...

...OR EVEN THE **FULL** EXTENT OF HIS POWERS!

OF COURSE WITH THE BOY DEEPLY ENTRENCHED IN AN AVENGERS TRAINING COMPLEX, THE POWER BROKER SAW VERY FEW WAYS TO MAKE AN OVERT **PROFIT** OFF OF HIM.

SO HE SOLD HARDBALL'S CONTRACT TO US.

USING IT AS LEVERAGE, IT WAS A SIMPLE MATTER TO MAKE THE BOY OUR PUPPET. HE'S ALREADY DONE ONE JOB FOR US. AND HE'S GETTING IN DEEPER.

THAT'S ALL WELL AND GOOD, BUT INEVITABLY HIS DOUBLE AGENT STATUS WILL BE COMPROMISED. WHAT THEN?

THEN, MY FRIENDS?

SNAP

VREEEET

WE NEED NOT **ALWAYS** CUT OFF A LIMB...

...TO ADD ANOTHER.

HAIL HYDRA.

HARDBALL IN

"BE ALL THAT YOU CAN BE"

MEMO
FROM: Baron Wernher von Blitzschlag
TO: Secretary Henry P. Gyrich
Personal and Confidential

Herr Gyrich: Per your request, I am compiling what I have learned about Michael van Patrick, code-named MVP.

As you know, the majority of my life has been spent in pursuit of creating der übermensch--what you Americans call "the super-soldier."

After Mr. van Patrick's unfortunate accident, I finally found myself with the opportunity to *dissect* one. To my surprise, I found...*nothing.*

For years I labored for the Reich to create übermenschen such as Master Man, Warrior Woman, and Vunder Knight.

To my shame, none of them held a candle to your country's Kapitan Amerika...

...or, for that matter, the genetic potential of this young man.

And I had no idea why. Why the family of this ordinary American boy should have succeeded where my genius failed.

Fortunately, in this age of marvels, one need not be a hen to lay an *egg.*

MVP IN

"BORN TO SERVE"

#8

IT'S ALL MY FAULT.

GOT TO STAY SMALL. IF I GROW I'LL MOVE FASTER, BUT I'LL BE A BIGGER TARGET. AND IF I'M A BIGGER TARGET I'M *DEAD*.

OH, LORD. I'M STEPPING IN HIS BLOOD. THIS CADET'S BEEN *BLOWN APART* AND I'M WALKING IN HIS--

NO, DON'T LOOK. KEEP MOVING. GOT TO REACH THE OUTSIDE...CALL FOR HELP.

WE'VE GOT OVER SIXTY SUPER HEROES ON BASE AND IT'S *NOT ENOUGH*. NOT *NEARLY* ENOUGH...

FACE IT, HANK. THIS IS THE *END OF THE INITIATIVE*.

MAYBE IT NEVER SHOULD HAVE STARTED. MAYBE THIS PROVES IT. AND IF THAT'S THE CASE, THERE'S NO QUESTION ABOUT WHO TO BLAME.

AFTER ALL... THIS WAS *YOUR* BRILLIANT IDEA...

OKAY, MAGGOTS—OFF THE BUS AND FALL IN!

HOLY CRAP. I THOUGHT I'D SEEN SOME MOPES IN MY DAY, BUT YOU ALL MAKE THE STILT-MAN LOOK LIKE DR. DOOM!

LET'S SEE. ANT-MAN...THE CRUSADER...MELEE...GELDOFF? GOT TIRED OF ORGANIZING LIVE AID CONCERTS, HUH?

DRAGON LORD...GEIGER...RED 9...AND DIAMONDBACK. FINALLY, SOMEONE I RECOGNIZE.

DRAGON LORD! POWERS AND ABILITIES.

I CAN SUMMON AND CONTROL DRAGONS, SIR.

YEAH? WHERE WERE YOU FIVE MINUTES AGO?

I HAVE TO MIX A BREW IN ONE OF MY SPECIAL CAULDRONS FIRST.

SON, THAT'S NOT A SUPER POWER. THAT'S HOME ECONOMICS.

MELEE. ACCORDING TO THE FILE, YOUR POWER'S A MASTERY OF EVERY FORM OF MARTIAL ARTS.

I'LL BE PAYING SPECIAL ATTENTION TO YOU, PRINCESS.

WAIT A SECOND... ANT-MAN?

ANT-MAN?

IF YOU'RE THE *SAME* ANT-MAN WHO BUSTED UP MY *CIRCUS* OPERATION--

SIR, NO SIR! I NEVER EVEN *MET* THAT LOSER!

BUT--BUT I HEARD *STORIES* ABOUT HIM!

LIKE...THEY WOULDN'T LET HIM JOIN THE *AVENGERS,* 'CAUSE HE WAS SO LAME, SO...HE HID IN THE MANSION AND *PRETENDED* TO BE ON THE TEAM!

...SO HE'S SITTING IN THE SHOWERHEAD, WATCHING *MS. MARVEL* SOAP UP! I MEAN, WHAT A *PERV,* RIGHT?

HAH! WAIT'LL I TELL THE GUYS!

STOP IT...

CASSIE-- NFF!

STOP TELLING LIES ABOUT MY *DAD!*

UH-OH.

THOOM THOOM THOOM

Briefing Room One.
Later.

ALL RIGHT, CADETS--DAMN IT, GYRICH, I CAN BARELY FEEL MY ARM! --LET'S DISCUSS YOUR MOST RECENT MISSION.

TRIATHLON-- HOW WOULD YOU EVALUATE YOUR STUDENTS?

I WAS EXTREMELY IMPRESSED. THERE WAS NO LOSS OF LIFE OR MAJOR PROPERTY DAMAGE.

IN FACT, GIVEN HER PERFORMANCE AGAINST DRAGON MAN, HYDRA AND OTHERS, I'D LIKE TO NOMINATE KOMODO FOR A COMMENDATION.

A WHAT? ARE YOU OUT OF YOUR MIND?

YOUR TEAM JUST LOST A VERY PUBLIC BATTLE AGAINST THE ZODIAC.* THE NEW WARRIORS-- OF ALL PEOPLE--HAD TO BAIL YOU OUT!

*IN NEW WARRIORS #4 --TOM.

TO MAKE MATTERS WORSE, ONE OF THE NEW WARRIORS WAS KILLED-- WHILE YOU WERE ON THE SCENE! THAT SHOULDN'T HAPPEN WHEN THE INITIATIVE'S AROUND!

UNTIL THEN WE HAD A PERFECT RECORD OF NO LOSSES!

WHY, I'VE GOT HALF A MIND TO MAKE YOU REPEAT YOUR INSTRUCTOR'S TRAINING--

SHUT UP!!

I HEAR ONE MORE WORD OUTTA YOU, OLD MAN, AND I'LL TELL EVERYONE YOUR "PERFECT RECORD'S" A LOAD OF CRAP!

YOU THINK YOU'RE THE ONLY ONE WHO CAN HOLD PEOPLE'S MISTAKES OVER THEM? WELL, THINK AGAIN!

YOU GOT SKELETONS IN YOUR CLOSET TOO. AND ONE OF 'EM'S A KILLER.

WHEN YOU'RE LIKE THIS-- Y'KNOW, ALL *LIZARDY*-- YOUR TONGUE'S KINDA ROUGH, AND YOUR CLAWS--

I GUESS WHAT I'M TRYING TO SAY IS, COULDN'T YOU CHANGE BACK TO NORMAL?

I...I CAN'T.

I'VE GOT THIS... *SECRET*...

I KNOW. I LIED BEFORE. I SAW YOU--*ALL OF YOU*-- WHEN YOU CHANGED BACK ON THAT FLIGHT FROM TEXAS.

I KNOW WHY YOU STOLE DOC CONNORS' LIZARD FORMULA.

AND...AND YOU'RE *OKAY* WITH IT?

HEY, I'M HERE, AREN'T I?

GO ON. I'LL HOLD YOU.

O-OKAY.

THERE WE GO.

LOOK AT YOU. YOU'RE BEAUTIFUL.

Y-YOU'RE *REALLY* OKAY WITH THIS?

HEY, TRUST ME.

WE'RE *ALL* DAMAGED GOODS.

WHAT WAS I *THINKING*? WHAT WERE *ANY* OF US--

YELLOWJACKET.

OH, NO...

...IT'S UNDERSTANDABLE, ABBY. EVERYTHING WE SEE AT THE INITIATIVE. ALL THIS DEATH AND DESTRUCTION? IT'D FREAK ANYBODY OUT.

HE'S STILL IN A COMA. LOOK, I'M SORRY WE HAVE TO DO THIS HERE. THE DOCS ARE GONNA LET ME OUT ANY DAY NOW.

BUT PLEASE, I THINK WE WERE MAKING PROGRESS.

TO BE HONEST, TRAUMA, I NEVER THOUGHT ABOUT IT MUCH BEFORE...

...UM... ARE YOU SURE THE GAUNTLET CAN'T HEAR US?

WELL...BEFORE I CAME HERE, I HADN'T LOST ANYONE CLOSE TO ME, NEVER MIND KILLED ANYONE. SO WHEN I SHOT DOWN THAT HYDRA AGENT, I--

--I MEAN, I KNOW HE WAS A BAD PERSON. BUT--

DON'T TELL ME. TELL HIM.

I...I DON'T REGRET SHOOTING YOU. YOU WERE A TERRORIST, TRYING TO KILL THE PRESIDENT. I HAD TO DO IT; I KNOW THAT.

BUT...BUT YOU WERE SOMEBODY'S SON. A REAL PERSON! AND I--

...AND OH GOD, I AM SO SORRY...

PERFECT. IN HIS STUDIES AS A THERAPIST. AND IN THE CONTROL OF HIS POWERS.

IT LOOKS LIKE YOUR WORK HERE IS DONE, DANI.

OH--MISTRESS MOONSTAR. I WISHED TO VISIT TRAUMA, BUT IF HE IS OCCUPIED--

NO, IT'S OKAY; HE'S JUST FINISHING UP WITH CLOUD 9.

"MISTRESS MOONSTAR?"

KROOOM

I KNOW THIS PLACE.

THIS IS WHERE I DIED.

UM... GELDOFF, IS THIS PART OF THE EXERCISE?

BEATS ME. BUT YOU'RE SUPPOSED TO CALL ME *PROTON* WHEN WE'RE TRAINING.

I THINK IT'S STUPID, BUT IF ANYONE CARED WHAT *I* THINK, I WOULDN'T EVEN *BE* HERE.

SCREW IT. THIS ROOM'S FOR KICKING ASS. YOU COME IN, YOU GOT AN ASS, IT GETS KICKED.

IS--IS THAT AN EARTHQUAKE?

WE WOULDN'T FEEL AN EARTHQUAKE-- THIS IS THE MOST HEAVILY REINFORCED LEVEL ON BASE. WHATEVER THAT WAS, IT HAPPENED CLOSE BY.

BRRRMMM

WE TWO ARE THE MIGHTIEST IN CAMP. IT FALLS TO US TO INVESTIGATE.

WHAT CAN I DO?

A CALLOW YOUTH SUCH AS YOU WOULD BE DESTROYED BY SO POTENT A FORCE. TAKE TO THE WINDS; ALERT THE OTHERS.

AND BE CAREFUL.

LOOK, I KNOW YOU THINK I'M ALL BUTCH OR SOMETHING. AND I'LL HELP IF I CAN. BUT--I'M NOT LIKE YOU, TARENE. REALLY!

NONSENSE! MINE OWN EYES BEHELD YOU DISPATCH A STONE MAN FROM SATURN AND HOLD THE HULK AT BAY!

TRULY, YOU WERE BORN TO THE BATTLEFIELD. TOGETHER, NO ENEMY--BE HE MORTAL OR GOD-- CAN HOPE TO WITHSTAND OUR POWER!

MR. SECRETARY, I THINK SOMETHING'S HAPPENING ON ONE OF THE SUBBASEMENTS.

I CAN SEE THAT, IDIOT.

The War Room.

BRRMM

SIR, WE JUST LOST OUR FEED TO ALL THE LOWER LEVELS!

SECRETARY GYRICH! THE NETWORK! IT'S BEEN COMPROMISED. ALL WE'RE GETTING IS THIS RECURSIVE LOOP! SHOULD WE CALL IN STARK? OR MAYBE CALL THE AVENGERS?

NEGATIVE. WE HAVE OVER SIXTY SUPERHUMANS ON BASE. WE DO NOT NEED ANYONE ELSE!

MY HAND... GOT TO FIND MY--

QUIET, DAMN IT! HE'LL HEAR--

STOP.

YOU'RE THE INSTRUCTOR?

UH... TECHNICALLY.

THEY WEREN'T READY FOR A LIVE FIREFIGHT. YOU WERE INCREDIBLY CARELESS WITH THEIR LIVES. YOU--

HANG ON A MINUTE.

UM...

WHAT IN THE @#*%? IS HE GONNA SLAG ME OR NOT?

HE SURE IS TAKIN' HIS SWEET TIME. JUST WHO IS HE TALKIN' TO OUT THERE? PYM?

YELLOWJACKET. YOU'RE ON MY LIST.

ZZRAKK

ONE WILL DIE!

#10

THIS IS MY SUPER SOAKER. THERE ARE MANY LIKE IT. BUT THIS ONE IS MINE! I CALL HER SHIRLEY.

SLAPSTICK! STEVE! WILL YOU GROW UP ALREADY! DEBRII WAS SAYING SOMETHING.

IT'S OKAY, ULTRAGIRL. I JUST IGNORE HIM. LISTEN, WE ALL SAW JUSTICE TAKE OFF WITH CLOUD 9...

AND EVERYBODY KNOWS SHE CAME BACK--AND HE DIDN'T. THE RUMOR IS HE'S GONE ROGUE. AND NOW EVERYBODY'S LOOKING AT US.

ALL I'M SAYIN' IS IT'S NOT A GOOD TIME TO BE AN EX-NEW WARRIOR.

THAT'S MY FAULT. EVERYONE THINKS IT WAS ME WHO BEAT THE GAUNTLET INTO A COMA.

IT'S ONLY A MATTER A' TIME BEFORE THEY WASH ME OUT, USE THE S.P.I.N. TECH TO TAKE MY POWERS AWAY, OR THROW ME IN JAIL.

UM, RAGE, ABOUT THAT... FUNNY STORY, Y'SEE I...

I SWEAR, I EVER CATCH THE GUY WHO REALLY DID IT...

...I'LL BEAT THE LIVING @#%* OUT A' HIM!

YOIKS!

C'MON, GUYS. THIS'S ALL IN YOUR MINDS. THERE'S NOTHING TO WORRY ABOUT.

MS. MARVEL JUST PUT ME IN CHARGE OF THE JUNIOR GUARDSMEN PROGRAM*. THAT WOULDN'T'VE HAPPENED IF THEY DIDN'T TRUST US.

*IN NEW WARRIORS #7 --TOM

OKAY. HERE'S THE THING. THERE'S SOMETHING I GOTTA TELL YOU.

HOLD UP, I THINK SLAPSTICK'S ACTUALLY GOT SOMETHING TO SAY. WHAT IS IT, STEVE?

IT WAS ME WHO--

BEEP BEEP

"BEEP BEEP?" WHAT AM I, A ROADRUNNER?

Camp Hammond
Cadet Barracks Bravo.
Now.

STUPID CLOUD! FASTER, C'MON!

GOTTA ROUND UP THE TROOPS! GET REINFORCEMENTS!

GUYS! IT'S AN EMERGENCY! SOUND THE ALARMS! ARM YOURSELVES AND FOLLOW ME!

SOMETHING BIG IS GOING ON DOWN IN THE LOWER LEVELS! AND WE'RE GONNA NEED EVERY LAST ONE OF...

...YOU?

GUYS? HARDBALL? RAGE? ANYONE HERE? MAYBE THEY'RE ALL ON THE GIRLS' SIDE...

ULTRAGIRL? KOMO--MO--MO

OH MY GOD!

CLOUD 9! GET OUT!

OH BOY.

LISTEN, IT'S NOT WHAT IT LOOKS LIKE! WE WEREN'T... FRATERNIZING, OR WHATEVER IT IS YOU'RE NOT SUPPOSED TO DO.

WHAT DID YOU SEE, YOU LITTLE SNEAK? AND WHAT WERE YOU DOING SPYING ON US?

I DIDN'T SEE ANYTHING, KOMODO AND Y'KNOW WHAT? IT DOESN'T MATTER!

WE'RE UNDER ATTACK! SOMETHING'S RUNNING AROUND IN THE SUBBASEMENTS AND FROM THE SOUND OF THINGS...

FEH! I AM BARON VON BLITZSCHLAG, UND I HAFF SEEN FAR VORSE. THIS IS NO TIME TO VEEP LIKE A LITTLE GIRL.

IF THE INITIATIVE IS TO SURVIVE... THERE IS VORK TO BE DONE.

The War Room.

KRASHH

RRRAAA!

FIRE!!

BUDDA BUDDA BUDDA

ALL OF YOU! KILLED IN ACTION!!

ZAK ZAK ZAK

Outside Camp.

WE'RE ALL GONNA DIE!

I KNEW THIS WOULD HAPPEN! THEY *HAD* TO PUT THIS BASE IN *OUR* CITY.

SHUT UP AND *RUN!*

ARGH!

HNGH!

KILLED... IN...ACTION!

BRRRT

ZAK

ZAK

OH MY GOD, MELATI!

RELAX, BLONDIE. I REGENERATE, REMEMBER? BUT IT'S NICE TO KNOW I'M MORE THAN A PRETTY FACE TO YOU.

WE CAN'T STAY OUT IN THE OPEN. C'MERE.

OW! STILL GOT A *HOLE* IN MY STOMACH HERE, GENIUS!

OUR ONLY HOPE IS THIS DEVICE. VE MUST REPROGRAM K.I.A.'S BRAIN PATTERNS...

VITH THOSE UFF MVP...BUT THOSE RECORDINGS VERE LOST VHEN THE LAB VAS DESTROYED.

YOU MUST *FULLY* DOWNLOAD THE BRAIN PATTERNS FROM THE MIND UFF A *HEALTHY* MICHAEL VAN PATRICK.

LIKE THE SCARLET SPIDERS?

YOU MEAN THE MVPEOPLE?!

NEIN...I AM ASHAMED TO SAY THE SPIDERS ARE IMPERFECT. I MIXED SOME UFF MY *OWN* DNA INTO THEIR GENETIC MAKEUP.

...

VHAT? I AM NINETY YEARS OLD. MY CLOCK VAS TICKING.

FOR THIS TO VORK, YOU VILL NEED THE **REAL** MVP.

THE **REAL--?**

BUT HE'S **DEAD.** YOU HAD HIS BODY IN YOUR LAB.

UND HOW DID YOU KNOW THAT, JUENGLING?

THAT'S **NOT** IMPORTANT! HOW DO WE **FIND** MVP?

YOU'RE TALKING ABOUT THE ONE WHO LIVES WITH HIS DAD, RIGHT? HE **WAS** IN ENTUCKY. BUT NOW HE'S **GONE!**

SUCH VELL-INFORMED CHILDREN. BUT YOUR ELDERS HAFF TRICKS OF THEIR OWN.

I HAD A CHIP IMPLANTED INTO HERR VAN PATRICK. THIS TRACKER VILL LEAD YOU DIRECTLY TO HIM.

WE'VE GOT TO MAKE A RUN FOR THE NEGATIVE ZONE JUMP GATE. IT'S THE ONLY WAY WE CAN GET TO MVP IN TIME.

GREAT.

THAT'S ON THE OTHER SIDE OF THE COMPOUND. WE'LL NEED COVER. I'LL USE MY CLOUDS LIKE A SMOKE-SCREEN...

I CAN TAKE THE POINT, TRY TO BLOCK ANY FIRE. IF I'M HIT, I SHOULD BE ABLE TO REGENERATE MOST DAMAGE.

I DON'T LIKE IT, BUT I DON'T HAVE ANY BETTER IDEAS. ON MY MARK...

GO!!

#11

THERE, COMMANDER RHODES. YOU'RE BACK UP. CAN YOU STAND ON YOUR OWN, SIR?

ABOUT...ALL I CAN DO. MY MASK...CAN'T BREATHE...TAKE IT OFF...

BUT, SIR, DIRECTOR STARK SAID...

DO IT!

SECRETARY GYRICH, WAR MACHINE IS DOWN, COPY?

HOLD ON, COMMANDER RHODES. WE HAVE MEDIC TRAINING, WE'LL--

--HELP... YOU...

COMMANDER? ARE YOU--

DON'T WASTE TIME ON HIM! PROCEED TO TENNESSEE AND ENGAGE THE ENEMY!

WRONG, GYRICH. YOU'VE THROWN ENOUGH KIDS AT THIS PROBLEM.

IT'S TIME TO BRING IN PROFESSIONALS. I'M CALLING TONY.

RHODES, YOU KEEP STARK OUT OF THIS! YOU-- ﹛SQUARK﹜

WAR MACHINE CALLING S.H.I.E.L.D.--WE HAVE AN OMEGA LEVEL THREAT. MY COMBAT SYSTEMS ARE DISABLED. I NEED BACKUP ASAP.

YOU SCARLET SPIDERS STICK AROUND. TONY WILL WANT YOU TO BRIEF HIM ON--

BLAST IT! THEY WENT INTO STEALTH MODE. ANYONE SEE WHERE THEY--?

SIR, LOOK--

--THE JUMP GATE'S POWERED UP!

DAMN...

#12

Camp Hammond.

The Gauntlet

LOOK AT YOU, SO HANDSOME! WE SHOULD TAKE SOME FAMILY PICTURES. PUT THE KIDS IN THEIR SUNDAY CLOTHES...

I'M GLAD TO BE BACK WITH YOU TOO, BABY.

BUT THIS IS NO TIME TO BE CELEBRATING.

Cloud 9

Yellowjacket

Komodo

Secretary Henry Peter Gyrich

Hardball

War Machine

Trauma

CHANGING OF THE GUARD

GENTLEMEN.

PLEASE COME IN.

HANK, IT'S GREAT TO SEE YOU LOOKING SO WELL. FOR A FEW HOURS THERE WE THOUGHT KIA HAD KILLED YOU.

SORRY. THE STRAIN OF SHRINKING TO SUBATOMIC SIZE SO FAST, ESPECIALLY WOUNDED, KNOCKED ME OUT FOR A WHILE.

YOU'RE GETTING PRETTY GOOD AT THE SUBATOMIC THING. THAT'S TWICE YOU'VE USED IT TO SAVE YOURSELF, RIGHT?

LET'S WAIT UNTIL THE HEARING'S OVER TO DECIDE IF I'VE SAVED MYSELF, OKAY, CAROL?

RHODEY, THIS COULD DRAG ON A WHILE. DO THE OTHERS KNOW ABOUT...YOUR **CONDITION?**

I'LL BE FINE, VAL. I'M DOING A LOT BETTER THAN I WAS AT O*N*E.

BUT NO, THEY DON'T. AND I'D LIKE TO KEEP IT THAT WAY.

SENATOR WOODMAN.

DON'T WORRY, HENRY, I'VE GOT YOUR BACK ON THIS. I'M NOT ABOUT TO LET THEM PIN THE OTHERS' INCOMPETENCE ON YOU.

YOU'RE MY EYES AND EARS IN THIS PLACE. AND I'M GOING TO MAKE DAMN SURE IT STAYS THAT WAY.

RRRMMM

GENTLEMEN, LADIES. SORRY I'M LATE--I HAD TO DEAL WITH A PRESSING S.H.I.E.L.D. MATTER.

IN FACT, THERE'S ALWAYS A PRESSING S.H.I.E.L.D. MATTER. SO IF YOU DON'T MIND--

--I'D LIKE TO CALL THIS TO ORDER.

I. MAN

FOR THE RECORD, I AM DIRECTOR ANTHONY STARK, A.K.A. IRON MAN, REPRESENTING S.H.I.E.L.D. ALSO PRESIDING ARE MS. MARVEL FOR THE AVENGERS, VALERIE COOPER OF O*N*E, AND, FOR THE SUPERHUMAN ARMED FORCES, SENATOR ARTHUR WOODMAN.

LADIES AND GENTLEMEN, WE'RE HERE TO DISCUSS A NUMBER OF DISTURBING EVENTS THAT HAVE RECENTLY COME TO LIGHT. CHIEF AMONG THESE IS THE DEATH OF AN INITIATIVE CADET, MVP, AND ITS SUBSEQUENT COVER-UP.

MR. GYRICH, YOU WERE PRESENT DURING THE TRAINING EXERCISE THAT CLAIMED THE BOY'S LIFE. WHAT HAPPENED?

ER   I. MAN   W

I DON'T RECALL.

YOU...DON'T RECALL.

MACHINE   GYRICH   PYM

I ASSUME YOU RECALL THE MORE RECENT DEATHS, DURING THE "KIA" INCIDENT.

EIGHT DECORATED S.H.I.E.L.D. AGENTS, ONE OF THE SCARLET SPIDERS, TERRANCE WARD, A.K.A. TRAUMA, AND ONE OF OUR NEWEST RECRUITS, TAKO SHAMARA, A.K.A. DRAGON LORD.

MRS. SHAMARA, ON BEHALF OF THE PRESIDENT, THE INITIATIVE, AND A GRATEFUL NATION, PLEASE ACCEPT THIS FLAG...

...AS A SYMBOL OF OUR APPRECIATION FOR YOUR LOVED ONE'S SERVICE.

YER FATHER HAD SPECIFIC WISHES ABOUT THE HANDLING OF HIS REMAINS. UM. HERE.

AWW...HE'S ALL MIXED UP IN A JAR. HE WOULDA LIKED THAT.

ANT-MAN!

THANK YOU, SIR. I WANT YOU TO KNOW THAT I INTEND TO HONOR MY FATHER BY TAKING UP HIS MANTLE.

I SHALL MASTER THE ART OF DRAGON SUMMONING. AND ONE DAY SOON, I WILL JOIN YOUR RANKS MYSELF!

GREAT. WE BETTER STOCK UP ON MORE JARS.

QUIET, TASKMASTER. DON'T MAKE ME TRIGGER THE NANOBOTS IN YOUR SYSTEM AND FRY YOUR BRAIN!

NOT THAT I'D MIND. BUT WE'VE HAD ENOUGH DEATHS AT CAMP HAMMOND ALREADY...

YOU ALL READY?

JUST... CAN I HAVE A SECOND, PLEASE?

SO, UH, SIR... YOU'RE OUT OF YOUR COMA. HOW'D YOU PULL THAT OFF?

I DIDN'T. IT WAS KIA'S WEAPON, THE TACTIGON. IT'S PROGRAMMED TO FIND AN ENEMY'S ACHILLES HEEL.

AND WHEN IT WAS FIGHTING ME, I WAS STILL OUT OF IT. MY GAUNTLET WAS DOING ALL THE WORK ON AUTOMATIC.

SO THE TACTIGON CREATED A DRUG THAT WOKE ME UP. IN ORDER TO WIN, IT FOUND THE GAUNTLET'S WEAKNESS.

AND THAT WAS ME. I WAS THE WEAKNESS, CADET.

SERGEANT, YOU CAN'T THINK LIKE THAT.

OKAY. I'M READY.

LOOK, WE THOUGHT WE LOST YOU. IF THE TACTIGON FOUND A WAY TO BRING YOU BACK...

...THEN THAT'S THE ONE GOOD THING THAT'S COME OUT OF ALL OF THIS.

IT'S NOT ENOUGH. NOT BY HALF. BECAUSE OF THAT WEAPON I'VE LOST TWO MEN UNDER MY WATCH. FIRST MVP...

...AND NOW TRAUMA.

THOR GIRL?

HOW LONG HAVE YOU BEEN HERE?

I HAVE NEVER LEFT HIS SIDE.

TRAUMA FELL DEFENDING ME. NOW I SERVE AS HIS SHIELD MAIDEN.

BY HIS SIDE SHALL I REMAIN, UNTIL THE *VALKYRIE* COME TO TAKE HIM TO VALHALLA.

I...SEE. WELL, I'M... SURE HE'D APPRECIATE THAT.

ARE WE IT? I THOUGHT--ISN'T ANYONE ELSE COMING?

THE VIEWING LASTS ALL DAY. THE WHOLE BASE WILL BE AT THE FUNERAL-- THE AVENGERS, TOO.

WHAT ABOUT CIVILIANS? WE SHOULD WEAR OUR MASKS IN FRONT OF TRAUMA'S FAMILY, RIGHT?

I DON'T THINK THAT'LL BE A PROBLEM. I GOT TO KNOW TRAUMA PRETTY WELL THESE PAST FEW WEEKS, AND...WELL...

...THERE'S A REASON HE'S BEING BURIED ON BASE. I DON'T THINK HIS FAMILY'S COMING. ANY OF THEM.

I CAN'T REALLY GET INTO DETAILS; HE WOULDN'T WANT ME TO. HE WAS PRETTY PRIVATE...

HHHUUUKK!

AAAA!

HELA'S BONES!

WHA--WHAT--

TERRY?

ARE YOU *NUTS*, CLOUD 9? HOW ARE YOU NOT FREAKING OUT?

HE *DIED!* THEY DID AN *AUTOPSY!*

THEY *EMBALMED* HIM!

GET WITH THE PROGRAM, KOMODO. THIS IS THE INITIATIVE. SO WHAT IS IT, TERRY? *CLONE? ROBOT? ZOMBIE? WHAT?*

I-I DON'T KNOW, ABBY. I MEAN, I'M *ME...*

...BUT I REALLY DON'T KNOW WHY I'M NOT DEAD.

:SIGH: SO *MR. GYRICH*, CAN YOU AT *LEAST* TELL US THE *NUMBER* OF INITIATIVE MEMBERS WHO WERE INJURED DURING THIS *FIASCO?*

I DON'T HAVE THE EXACT FIGURES.

UH, HOWEVER, WE *CAN* ASSURE YOU THEY'RE BEING WELL TAKEN CARE OF.

THE INFIRMARY'S TAKEN ON A NEW DEPARTMENT HEAD, CODENAMED *PHYSIQUE*, WHO SPECIALIZES IN SUPERHUMAN MEDICINE.

NIGHTHAWK'S THERE NOW, MA'AM, AWARDING CITATIONS TO OUR WOUNDED.

COOPER

MACHINE

GYRICH

Camp Hammond Infirmary.

GO ON IN, SIR. YOU'RE EXPECTED.

DOCTOR, I'M SORRY TO INTERRUPT, BUT I'M HERE TO PRESENT PURPLE HEARTS TO THE BRAVE MEN AND--

--UH... WOMEN...

IT'S QUITE ALL RIGHT, NIGHTHAWK; YOU REACTED BETTER THAN MOST DO WHEN THEY FIRST SEE ME.

PLEASE, COME IN; I WAS JUST CHECKING TO SEE HOW *THE CRUSADER'S* HAND FUNCTIONS, NOW THAT IT'S BEEN REATTACHED.

OF... COURSE. THEN IF I'M NOT INTERRUPTING, I'LL JUST, UH, PROCEED.

CONSTRICTOR, I CAN'T TELL YOU HOW SORRY I AM THAT YOU LOST YOUR ARMS. I'VE HAD...FRIENDS THAT'S HAPPENED TO.

IF IT'S ANY CONSOLATION, I THINK YOU PROVED ONCE AND FOR ALL THAT YOU'VE LEFT YOUR CRIMINAL PAST BEHIND. SO, ON BEHALF OF THE PRESIDENT--

THAT'S CLOSE ENOUGH, RICHMOND.

FRANK? IS SOMETHING WRONG?

WHAT--YOU THINK I'M MAD AT YOU FOR TALKING ME INTO JOINING THIS OUTFIT?

NAH. JUST WANTED TO TEST OUT MY NEW BIONIC ARMS--I DON'T EVEN NEED MY COILS ANYMORE, SEE?

BESIDES, LIKE YOU SAID, I'M LEGIT NOW. A CHANGED MAN.

AND WHAT'S A COUPLE OF LIMBS IN EXCHANGE FOR RESPECTABILITY, RIGHT?

UH...RIGHT. WELL... CONGRATULATIONS.

HOW'S THIS ONE DOING, DOC?

NO ILL EFFECTS. WHICH IS A BIT OF A SHOCK CONSIDERING...

...HIS SEVERED HAND WAS ALREADY GOING GREEN--

WELL, I AM A SHAPE-SHIFTER. IT'S EASY FOR ME TO REASSEMBLE MYSELF.

STILL, I'D LIKE TO DO A FULL BODY SCAN JUST TO PLAY IT SAFE. IF YOU'D PLEASE...

YOU'RE THE DOCTOR.

I WONDER. IS THEIR EARTH-SCIENCE ADVANCED ENOUGH...?

...COULD THIS PROCEDURE REVEAL MY TRUE IDENTITY?

I CAN'T TAKE THAT CHANCE. IF HUMAN AUTHORITIES FOUND OUT I WAS A SKRULL...

...THEY'D *NEVER* BELIEVE I'VE RENOUNCED MY PEOPLE, ESPECIALLY AFTER I'VE DECEIVED THEM FOR SO LONG.

NO NEED TO PANIC. THIS RING WAS MADE FROM FRAGMENTS OF THE *COSMIC CUBE*. WITHIN ITS IMMEDIATE PROXIMITY, THERE SHOULD BE NOTHING IT CAN'T DO--

--INCLUDING CHANGE ME FROM SKRULL TO HUMAN AT THE MOLECULAR LEVEL!

WELL, DOCTOR? SHOULD I BE WORRIED?

NO, YOU'RE COMPLETELY HEALTHY. IN FACT, I'VE *NEVER* SEEN READINGS SO PERFECTLY NORMAL ACROSS THE BOARD.

SURE, RUB IT IN.

GREAT NEWS. BUT YOU WERE STILL WOUNDED IN THE LINE OF DUTY, WHICH MEANS YOU EARNED THIS.

UND ME? VILL I BE RECEIVING A PURPLE HEART AS VELL?

LOOK AT ME. SURELY YOU CANNOT DENY THAT I HAFF SUFFERED IN THE LINE OF DUTY.

WELL, NO. BUT THE U.S. GOVERNMENT DOES NOT GIVE MEDALS TO *NAZIS*, BARON.

AH. BUT YOU ARE HAPPY TO *EMPLOY* THEM VHEN THEY CAN *HELP* YOU, EH?

FEH. THE *RED SKULL* DID NOT APPRECIATE ME EITHER.

LET'S MOVE ON, MR. GYRICH. I HAVE CONCERNS ABOUT THE INITIATIVE MEMBERS WHO ONCE BELONGED TO THE **NEW WARRIORS.** IS IT TRUE THEY'VE GONE AWOL?

I CAN'T RECALL, SENATOR. I WASN'T PRESENT DURING THEIR LAST FIELD MISSION.

TRUE ENOUGH. THANK YOU FOR YOUR TESTIMONY.

WOODMAN

MS. MARVEL

THANK HIM? FOR **WHAT?** HE HASN'T ANSWERED A SINGLE QUESTION!

PERHAPS **YOU** SHOULD ANSWER MY LAST QUESTION, IRON MAN. AFTER ALL, UNLIKE MR. GYRICH, **YOU WERE** THERE WHEN THE FORMER NEW WARRIORS BROKE RANKS.

ACCORDING TO SEVERAL ACCOUNTS, YOU TOOK NO ACTION TO STOP THEM. IS IT TRUE THAT, IN FACT, YOU PROMISED THEM A **HEAD START?**

OF ALL THE--

EASY, TONY. I DON'T LIKE HIS TONE EITHER, BUT IT'S A LEGITIMATE QUESTION.

I. MAN

WOODM

IF I MAY...ONE OF THOSE CADETS DID RETURN TO BASE.

GUARDS, IF YOU'LL LET HER IN, I'M CERTAIN SHE CAN SHED SOME LIGHT ON THE SUBJECT.

THE TRIBUNAL RECOGNIZES SUSANNA SHERMAN, A.K.A. ULTRAGIRL.

IT'S OKAY, SUZY. JUST TELL THE TRUTH AND YOU'LL DO FINE.

THANK YOU.

I GUESS IT STARTED RIGHT AFTER THE BATTLE...

Tennessee.

YOU ALL DID YOURSELVES PROUD AGAINST KIA, *JUSTICE*. LET'S HEAD BACK TO BASE AND WE'LL--

NO, IRON MAN...I CAN'T. NONE OF US CAN.

ALL THIS-- THE DEAD, THE WOUNDED-- NONE OF IT WOULD HAVE HAPPENED IF NOT FOR THE INITIATIVE. THE SECRETS, THE LIES, THE COVER-UPS...I WON'T BE A PART OF IT ANYMORE.

IF ANYTHING, I NEED TO ACTIVELY *OPPOSE* IT--MAKE SURE IT NEVER HAPPENS AGAIN. AND THE *ONLY* PEOPLE I'D TRUST TO HELP ME DO THAT ARE MY FRIENDS... THE *OLD* NEW WARRIORS.

WHAT ARE YOU TALKING ABOUT...SOME KIND OF *COUNTER- INITIATIVE?*

A *COUNTER FORCE.* SOMEONE TO KEEP AN EYE ON THE INITIATIVE, MAKE SURE IT DOESN'T ABUSE ITS POWER... AND *STOP* IT IF IT DOES.

I'M A LICENSED HERO. WE'RE ALL REGISTERED AND TRAINED. I'M NOT TALKING ABOUT BREAKING LAWS...BUT WE NEED AUTONOMY. AFTER TODAY, IRON MAN, YOU *OWE* US.

...

ONE DAY'S HEAD START. IF YOU DO ANYTHING ILLEGAL...

WE'LL TURN OURSELVES IN.

I WANT TO MAKE SURE YOU'RE ALL ON BOARD. THIS ISN'T THE INITIATIVE. NO ONE'S FORCING YOU TO DO ANYTHING.

WE'VE GOT YOUR BACK, VANCE. AND CAN I JUST SAY THAT IT'S ABOUT DAMN TIME.

GREAT. I JOINED THE NEW WARRIORS TO GET FAMOUS, AND NOW I'M GOING UNDERGROUND WITH A BUNCH OF VIGILANTE FUGITIVES!

BUT WHAT THE HELL. CAMO PANTS MAKE MY BUTT LOOK BIG.

THERE'S NO WAY I'M GOING ANYWHERE NEAR THE INITIATIVE. EVER AGAIN.

MVP IS OUR BROTHER. WHERE HE GOES, WE GO.

I STILL CAN'T BELIEVE THIS. YOU SCARLET SPIDERS WERE CLONED FROM MY SON?

YOU ALL LOOK IDENTICAL... HOW DO I EVEN KNOW WHICH ONE'S THE ORIGINAL?

IT...IT'S ME, DAD. I'M YOUR SON...I'M MICHAEL.

SLAPSTICK... IF WE'RE GOING UNDERCOVER, YOU PROBABLY OUGHT TO TAKE OFF YOUR MAGIC GLOVES. GO BACK TO LOOKING NORMAL FOR A WHILE.

UH...THE THING IS, RAGE... I HAVEN'T CHANGED BACK TO STEVE HARMON SINCE WE STARTED TRAINING. AND, Y'KNOW, I'VE NEVER BEEN SLAPSTICK FOR THIS LONG BEFORE.

SOMETHING'S GONE WRONG. I CAN'T TAKE THE GLOVES OFF. I'M STUCK LIKE THIS.

BUT THE REAL PROBLEM--

--I THINK I LIIIIIIIKE IT!

DON'T WORRY. I'VE GOT PLACES WE CAN GO--PLACES SO FAR OFF THE GRID, EVEN THE HIGH-AND-MIGHTY *TONY STARK* WON'T BE ABLE TO FIND THEM.

IT'S DECIDED, THEN. LET'S LEAVE BEFORE IRON MAN CHANGES HIS MIND.

...SUZY?

WHAT'S THE MATTER?

I CAN'T GO WITH YOU, VANCE.

I BELIEVE IN THE INITIATIVE. YES THEY'VE MADE MISTAKES, BUT I DON'T WANT TO RUN AWAY FROM THEM. I WANT TO TRY TO *FIX* THEM.

I WON'T TURN MY BACK ON ALL I'VE WORKED FOR...NOT EVEN FOR YOU. I'M SORRY.

SO AM I.

TAKE CARE OF YOURSELF, SUZY.

IT'S OKAY, DUDE. THE TWO OF YOU CAN BE "ENEMIES WITH BENEFITS."

SHUT UP, SLAPSTICK.

"THAT WAS THE LAST TIME I SAW THEM. I REMAIN COMMITTED TO THE INITIATIVE, BUT TO MY KNOWLEDGE, VANCE AND THE OTHERS HAVEN'T BROKEN ANY LAWS...

"...AND UNTIL THEY DO, AS FAR AS I'M CONCERNED, THEY HAVE THEIR LIVES... AND I HAVE MINE."

I KNOW IT'S HARD TO DO THE RIGHT THING WHEN YOUR FRIENDS CHOOSE A DIFFERENT PATH, BUT IF IT MEANS ANYTHING, I'M PROUD OF YOU.

THANKS, MS. MARVEL. THAT HELPS. A LOT.

SUZY... YOU CAN CALL ME CAROL.

WE'VE BEEN AT THIS A WHILE. WAR MACHINE, WOULD YOU LIKE TO TAKE A BREAK AT THIS TIME?

NO.

ARE YOU SURE? YOUR SUIT COULDN'T USE A... RECHARGE?

I SAID I'M FINE. CAN WE CONTINUE?

W. MACHINE

ALL RIGHT THEN...LET'S TALK ABOUT THE CLONES.

WHAT ON EARTH WERE YOU THINKING? AFTER THE PROBLEMS WE HAD WITH THE CLONE OF THOR, WHAT POSSESSED YOU TO CONTINUE CLONING SUPERHUMANS?

THAT'S JUST IT-- MICHAEL VAN PATRICK WASN'T A SUPERHUMAN. HE WAS THE PERFECT PHYSICAL SPECIMEN OF HUMANITY. WE HAD NO REASON TO EXPECT PROBLEMS.

AFTER ALL, THERE HAVE BEEN NUMEROUS SUCCESSFUL INSTANCES OF NON-SUPERHUMAN CLONING. AND WE DID CLEAR THIS THROUGH THE PROPER CHANNELS.

YOU WHAT--? I DIDN'T HEAR ABOUT--

HE'S RIGHT. THIS WAS ALL APPROVED THROUGH THE SUPERHUMAN ARMED FORCES. WE HAVE FIFTY STATES TO FILL WITH INITIATIVE TEAMS-- HOW ELSE ARE WE SUPPOSED TO STAFF THEM ALL?

AND NO ONE THOUGHT TO CONSULT ME ON THIS?

TOO BAD BLITZSCHLAG'S NOT HERE. HE COULD TELL 'EM "VE VERE JUST FOLLOWING ORDERS."

WHAT WAS THAT, GYRICH?

SORRY, SIR...I DON'T RECALL.

ALL RIGHT, I'VE JUST ABOUT HAD IT WITH YOU.

YEAH? WELL, I'VE HAD IT WITH YOU ASKING ALL THE QUESTIONS WHEN I HAVE A FEW FOR YOU.

THE AVENGERS RECOVERED KIA'S BODY, BUT IT WASN'T RETURNED TO THE INITIATIVE.

SO?

SO WHERE'S THE TACTIGON?

KIA'S WEAPON?

THE DEADLIEST WEAPON IN THE UNIVERSE! IT'S INITIATIVE PROPERTY! WHERE IS IT?!

LET ME THINK...

SORRY. I CAN'T RECALL.

YOU SELF-RIGHTEOUS @#%*! WHAT GIVES YOU THE RIGHT? MVP? THAT KID WAS A NOBODY. A PAWN. YOU'VE GOT THE BLOOD OF CAPTAIN AMERICA ON YOUR HANDS, STARK!

THAT'S IT, GYRICH. NO MATTER WHAT ELSE HAPPENS AT THIS TRIBUNAL, I CAN PROMISE ONE THING--YOU'RE GONE!

ME?! I'VE GOT CONNECTIONS IN THE C.S.A., O*N*E, S.A.F., AND THE WHITE HOUSE! IF ANYONE'S GONE IT'S YOU! YOU AND YOUR S.H.I.E.L.D. INTERFERENCE!

C'MON! LET'S CALL THE OVAL OFFICE RIGHT NOW! YOU'LL SEE! I'M NOT GOING ANYWHERE!!

...AND SO, AFTER A GREAT DEAL OF THOUGHT AND SOUL-SEARCHING...

...I'VE DECIDED TO LEAVE THE INITIATIVE IN ORDER TO SPEND MORE TIME WITH MY FAMILY.

SALLY FLOYD, *FRONT LINE.*

MR. GYRICH...YOU DON'T *HAVE* A FAMILY.

NO MORE QUESTIONS. THANK YOU.

GOD, I HATE THAT WOMAN.

THANK YOU FOR COMING. IN LIGHT OF RECENT EVENTS, I REALIZE THERE'S SOMETHING I MUST *CONFESS* TO ALL OF YOU.

I HAVEN'T PUT AS MUCH FOCUS ON THE INITIATIVE AS I SHOULD HAVE. THOSE DAYS ARE OVER.

THAT SAID, I HAVE TO ADMIT THAT THIS *PROGRAM* HASN'T MET WITH MANY OF MY EXPECTATIONS.

HOWEVER, I CONSIDER MYSELF FORTUNATE--

--FORTUNATE THAT THIS GRADUATING *CLASS* HAS EXCEEDED THEM!

"THESE CADETS WERE THRUST INTO CHALLENGING, OFTEN FRIGHTENING SITUATIONS...

"...WITH NO IDEA OF WHAT TO EXPECT, BECAUSE NO ONE HAD DONE IT BEFORE.

"THEY FACED OVERWHELMING ODDS WITH COURAGE AND DIGNITY.

"AND WHEN THOSE WITH MORE EXPERIENCE FELL SHORT OF THE MARK...

"...THEY'VE RISEN TO THE NOBLEST IDEALS BEHIND THE INITIATIVE PROGRAM...

"...AND THE PROUD TRADITION OF THE GREAT HEROES WHO INSPIRED US ALL."

I'M USUALLY NOT ONE TO GET NOSTALGIC...BUT I HAVE TO SAY, SUZY, SEEING YOU IN MY OLD COSTUME MAKES ME INCREDIBLY PROUD.

IT MAKES ME INCREDIBLY NERVOUS. I'M NOT SURE I CAN LIVE UP TO IT.

TAKE IT FROM THE NEW 3-D MAN--THE BEST WAY TO HONOR A LEGACY IS TO CREATE YOUR OWN.

NOW C'MON-- WE'VE GOT A GRADUATION TO GET TO.

#13

#13 VARIANT

YOU *HAPPY* ABOUT THAT, *POPCORN?* TAKE A LOOK OUTSIDE. FOLKS AROUND HERE DON'T THINK TOO HIGHLY OF US.

AHH, THEY'RE JUST SCARED. ONCE THEY SEE HOW WE PROTECT 'EM, THEY'LL COME AROUND.

OH, AND MY NAME'S NOT *POPCORN,* IT'S *BOULDER.* MY SECRET IDENTITY'S EMERY SCHAUB. I'M FROM MORGANTON, NORTH CAROLINA. THAT'S NEAR ASHEVILLE.

YOU'RE *PRODIGY,* RIGHT? I SAW YOU FIGHT IRON MAN ON TV. REMEMBER WHEN HE ZAPPED YOU WITH HIS REPULSORS? THAT WAS AWESOME.

ACTUALLY, I DON'T REMEMBER MUCH OF IT. I WAS PRETTY DRUNK.

LOOK, I'M ONLY HERE BECAUSE I COULDN'T TAKE ANOTHER DAY IN JAIL. SO PARDON ME IF I DON'T SHARE YOUR ENTHUSIASM, PAL.

OH JEEZ, AN' I *GOTTA* KNOW WHO YOU ARE, *ANNEX!* I'VE ONLY BEEN TRYING TO WORK UP THE NERVE TO SAY HI THE WHOLE *TRIP!*

YEAH, THAT MAKES TWO OF US.

HECK, YOU GOT *TONS OF* EXPERIENCE. AND YOU WERE IN THE ARMY BEFORE THAT. I'M SURPRISED THEY'RE MAKING YOU TRAIN AT ALL.

WILL YOU *PLEASE* GIVE IT A REST, CAPTAIN MAN-BOOBS? SOME OF US ARE ONLY HERE BECAUSE IT WAS EITHER THAT OR ROT IN *PRISON.*

AT LEAST MY CELL AT THE *VAULT* WAS QUIET.

DON'T LET **SUNSTREAK** GET TO YOU, MAN. SHE'S A VILLAIN, THEY'RE ALL LIKE THAT.

I'M BATWING.

SHOOT, I REMEMBER YOU! YOU FOUGHT SPIDER-MAN! I THOUGHT YOU GOT CURED.

YEAH, SO DID I. I'M KINDA HOPING THEY CAN HELP ME HERE. AT LEAST I CAN TALK BETTER THAN I USED TO.

THAT'S **GORILLA GIRL.**

MA'AM. SORRY, BUT I AIN'T NEVER HEARD OF YOU.

DON'T WORRY ABOUT IT. I KNOW I'M KIND OF OUT OF MY DEPTH. BUT THE JUDGE TOLD ME I HAD TO REGISTER, SO...

I JUST WANT TO GET MY DIPLOMA OR WHATEVER AND GO HOME.

TEN-**SHUN!** FOUNDING AVENGER ON DECK!

DOCTOR HENRY PYM.

ANT-MAN. GIANT-MAN. GOLIATH. **YELLOW-JACKET.**

THIS IS SO...I AM SO...

AT EASE, SON.

OH...MY... LORD.

AW, HECK... I MEAN...YOU WERE ONE OF THE FIRST GREAT MODERN HEROES. YOU HELPED *FOUND* THE *AVENGERS!*

≈COUGH≈WIFEBEATER.

YOU FOUGHT DR. DOOM. YOU FOUGHT THE HULK. YOU DISCOVERED PYM PARTICLES. YOU SAVED THE PRESIDENT FROM *HYDRA!* YOU'RE A *LEGEND!*

THERE'S SOMETHING I'VE ALWAYS WANTED TO ASK YOU.

THAT'S *ENOUGH*, KID, THIS AIN'T NO FAN CLUB.

IT'S *OKAY*, CHUCK. ASK AWAY, YOUNG MAN.

WHAT WAS IT LIKE, BEING THE ONE TO PULL CAPTAIN AMERICA OUT OF THE ICE?

ONE THING YOU SHOULD ALL REMEMBER: YOUR JOB IS TO KEEP YOUR EYES AND EARS *OPEN* AND YOUR MOUTHS *SHUT*.

YOU MIND DOING THE WELCOME SPEECH FOR ME, CHUCK? I'M...NOT FEELING WELL.

WHAT'D I SAY?

DUDE, THINK ABOUT IT. OF ALL THE POSSIBLE TOUCHY SUBJECTS--

ALL RIGHT, YOU WALKING WASTES OF TAXPAYER DOLLARS...

...FALL IN!

I'M THE TASKMASTER. AND I WILL BE YOUR DRILL INSTRUCTOR.

OVER THE NEXT FEW WEEKS, YOU'LL GO FROM HATING ME TO DESPISING ME TO LOATHING ME. I'LL GO FROM NOT CARING TO NOT GIVING A DAMN TO ENJOYING IT.

THE LAST GUY WHO DID THIS JOB WAS STRAIGHT-UP MILITARY--THE YELLING AND THE SCREAMING AND THE WHOLE "FULL METAL JACKET" THING. THAT AIN'T ME.

HERE'S MY WAY: YOU DO EXACTLY WHAT I SAY EXACTLY WHEN I SAY OR I MAKE YOU HURT UNTIL YOU DO. IS THAT UNDERSTOOD?

SIR, YES SIR!

YOU. WHAT'S YOUR CODE NAME?

BO--

WRONG!

YOU HAVE TO EARN THE RIGHT TO CHOOSE YOUR CODE NAME. UNTIL THEN, I PICK IT.

LET'S SEE... WHAT'S A GOOD ONE FOR YOU... AHA! GOT IT.

WELCOME TO THE INITIATIVE, BUTTERBALL.

ALL RIGHT, FORM UP. TEN MILE RUN.

NOT MUCH. THEY'RE **Z-LIST**, THE LOT OF 'EM. **ANNEX** HAS PROMISE, BUT HE THINKS HE ALREADY KNOWS EVERYTHING, WHICH MAKES HIM AN IDIOT.

"SEE FOR YOURSELF. I BORROWED THE **CONSTRICTOR** TO SEE HOW HE HANDLES ELECTRICITY. THAT'S ENOUGH JUICE TO FRY A RHINO; BUTTERBALL DOESN'T EVEN BLINK.

"HE CAN'T BE SHOT, STABBED, POISONED, DROWNED, SUFFOCATED, OR HARMED IN ANY OTHER CONVENTIONAL WAY WE CAN FIGURE.

"CAN'T EVEN BE HURT BY MENTAL ATTACKS...ALTHOUGH A TELEPATH COULD STILL CONTROL HIS MIND."

'COURSE, GIVE ME SOMETHING SHINY, AND SO CAN I. THE KID'S NOT A ROCKET SCIENTIST.

IF HE'S INDESTRUCTIBLE, HE DOESN'T HAVE TO BE.

I CONCUR WITH **WAR MACHINE**. IT SOUNDS LIKE HE'S MORE OF A BRUISER TYPE.

YOU'D THINK SO. THE THING IS...

"...HE'S NOT STRONG. HE'S NOT FAST. AND EVEN IF HE WASN'T BUILT LIKE A TUB OF PUDDING...

"...HE'D STILL BE A KLUTZ."

WHUMP

"WELL, BEFORE HE CAME HERE HE WAS A FRY COOK, NOT A NINJA. IT'S OUR JOB TO WHIP HIM INTO SHAPE."

"BELIEVE ME, I BEEN TRYING.

"HE DOESN'T GET TIRED. HE CAN RUN ALL DAY WITHOUT BREAKING A SWEAT... AT A SNAIL'S PACE, BUT HE CAN DO IT.

"SAME WITH WEIGHTLIFTING. ANYTHING REMOTELY HEAVY HE CAN'T BUDGE AT ALL, BUT HE CAN LIFT LIGHTER WEIGHTS 'TIL THE COWS COME HOME.

"HE'S NOT LOSING ANY FAT, AND HE'S NOT GETTING ANY STRONGER."

I HAVE A THEORY ABOUT THAT.

A SIDE EFFECT OF HIS INVULNERABILITY IS THAT HIS BODY DOESN'T CHANGE. HIS METABOLISM DOESN'T FUNCTION LIKE A NORMAL HUMAN'S.

EXERCISE WON'T HAVE ANY EFFECT. IN ESSENCE, THIS BOY IS "FROZEN" IN THE STATE HE WAS IN WHEN HIS POWERS ACTIVATED.

IN OTHER WORDS, HE'S A FAT WIMP FOREVER.

WELL, HE *EATS*...SO A NEAR-STARVATION DIET MIGHT CAUSE HIM TO LOSE WEIGHT. IN TWO OR THREE YEARS.

I GET THE FEELING THERE'S SOMETHING MORE BOTHERING YOU, TASKMASTER. IS HE A DISCIPLINE PROBLEM?

"OH, DON'T EVEN GET ME STARTED."

DON'T LET GO OF THE ARROW; JUST RELAX YOUR HAND. ANY QUESTIONS?

SSFHUNK

I HAVE ONE, MR. TASKMASTER, SIR.

I READ ON THE INTERNET THAT YOU ONLY HAVE TO SEE SOMETHING DONE ONCE, AND YOU CAN ALL OF A SUDDEN DO IT YOURSELF.

YEAH, THAT'S RIGHT. IT'S CALLED HAVING "PHOTOGRAPHIC REFLEXES." I CAN SHOOT LIKE HAWKEYE, FIGHT LIKE IRON FIST, FENCE LIKE THE BLACK KNIGHT.

YOU DON'T HAVE TO TRAIN OR PRACTICE OR ANYTHING?

NOPE. THERE A POINT TO THIS, BUTTERBALL?

SO, UM... THEN WHAT QUALIFIES YOU TO TEACH US HOW TO PRACTICE?

"I CAN'T PUNISH HIM BY MAKING HIM RUN LAPS, OR DO PUSH-UPS IN THE RAIN, OR ANY OF THE OTHER USUAL TRICKS.

"NORMALLY WHAT YOU DO IN THAT SITUATION IS PUNISH THE OTHERS.

"MOTIVATE THEM TO USE *PEER PRESSURE* TO MAKE THE MALCONTENT STRAIGHTEN UP."

I...I DON'T WANNA DO THIS. EMERY DOESN'T MEAN IT.

YEAH, WELL, I DON'T WANNA KEEP DOING PUSH-UPS 'TIL I PUKE.

SUNSTREAK'S RIGHT. THIS IS HOW WE DID IT IN THE SERVICE. IT'S THE ONLY WAY TO TURN SOME GUYS INTO TEAM PLAYERS.

ALL...ALL RIGHT. IF YOU SAY SO.

GOOD. OKAY, ON THREE. ONE...TWO...

THREE!

WHAP WHAP WHAP

SNXXXX

"BUT WE RAN INTO PROBLEMS THERE, TOO."

"I'M TELLIN' YA, NOTHING GETS TO THIS KID."

I'M SURE IT'S FRUSTRATING. BUT INVULNERABILITY IS TOO VALUABLE A POWER TO GO TO WASTE.

STUDY FOOTAGE OF FAT GUYS FIGHTING-- THE KINGPIN, THE BLOB, SUMO WRESTLERS--AND APPLY THE TECHNIQUES TO SCHAUB.

BUT THOSE GUYS ARE ALL STRONG--

ARE YOU ADMITTING FAILURE, TASKMASTER?

NO. SIR.

GOOD. NOW ON TO OTHER MATTERS. S.H.I.E.L.D. PICKED UP INTEL THAT THERE'S A CONTRACT OUT ON YOU. RETRIBUTION FOR COLLABORATING WITH THE ENEMY, AS IT WERE.

WE'LL INCREASE YOUR SECURITY, BUT I WANTED YOU TO KNOW. BE EXTRA CAREFUL.

YOU DON'T SEEM ESPECIALLY CONCERNED.

I'M NOT.

MIND TELLING US WHY?

'CAUSE BULLSEYE'S WITH THE THUNDERBOLTS...I HEAR ELEKTRA'S DEAD...AGAIN...

...AND THEY CAN'T SEND ME AFTER MYSELF.

UH...ALL RIGHT.

JIM, IF YOU HAVE A MINUTE, I'D LIKE TO GO OVER PREPARATIONS FOR PRODIGY'S PRESS CONFERENCE.

I WANT TO MAKE SURE HE WON'T BE TEMPTED TO TRY ANYTHING RASH...

COULD YOU *POSSIBLY* HAVE BEEN LESS CONVINCING? I CAN JUST *IMAGINE* WHAT JON STEWART'S GOING TO DO WITH THAT SOUND-BITE.

LAY OFF ME, DAMN IT! I DID EXACTLY WHAT YOU WANTED.

I GOT UP THERE AND CONFESSED TO A DRINKING PROBLEM I *DON'T HAVE*--

--WON'T *ADMIT* TO YOURSELF--

--AND SOLD *EVERYBODY* AND *EVERYTHING* I FOUGHT FOR IN THE CIVIL WAR DOWN THE *RIVER* LIKE A GOOD LITTLE *SELLOUT!*

PLENTY OF PEOPLE WHO FOUGHT ON YOUR SIDE HAVE ACCEPTED REGISTRATION. NO ONE ASKED YOU TO SELL OUT.

THAT'S *CRAP!* YOU WANTED TO PARADE ME IN FRONT OF THE REPORTERS AS A *TEAM PLAYER* 'CAUSE I WAS ONE OF THE MOST *VISIBLE* SYMBOLS OF THE RESISTANCE!

YOU HAD ME BY THE SHORT HAIRS AND YOU USED IT TO *FORCE* ME TO DANCE TO YOUR TUNE!

WE OFFERED YOU THE SAME CHANCE WE'VE OFFERED DOZENS OF OTHERS. NO ONE COERCED YOU INTO TAKING IT.

IF YOU FELT SO STRONGLY ABOUT THIS, YOU COULD ALWAYS HAVE STAYED IN PRISON. WITH THOSE WHO REFUSED TO COMPROMISE THEIR BELIEFS.

I'LL LET YOU GET AWAY WITH THAT *ONCE.* BUT *NEXT TIME*--

AHH, GO RIDE AN ANT.

THE BEST FIGHTS ARE.

RIGHT, AND GET CANCER. YOU'D LOVE THAT.

MAN, IT'S *DEAD* AROUND HERE TONIGHT. THE UPPERCLASSMEN ARE SO LUCKY, GETTING A FIELD TRIP TO AVENGERS TOWER.

I WISH *WE* COULD GO SOMEWHERE. I'M SICK OF THIS PLACE.

THAT'S IT!

...AND I SURE DO MISS MY CAT, SAM. *SPEEDBALL* HAD A CAT WITH THE SAME POWERS AS HIM. SAM DOESN'T HAVE POWERS, BUT HE CAN OPEN DOORS...

YOU GUYS EVER SEE "STRIPES"? PUT ON YOUR BEST CAMO PANTS, KIDS...

...BECAUSE WE ARE GOING OUT ON THE TOWN TONIGHT!

I DON'T KNOW ABOUT THIS, PRODIGY. WE'RE NOT SUPPOSED TO LEAVE BASE WITHOUT PERMISSION.

C'MON, EMERY. I THOUGHT YOU WANTED TO BE ONE OF THE GUYS.

I DO, BUT I DON'T WANT TO GET IN TROUBLE.

ANNEX IS JAMMING THE SECURITY CAMERAS. ALL WE HAVE TO DO IS MAKE SURE WE DON'T GET CAUGHT.

UM, THEY'VE GOT A LOT MORE THAN CAMERAS FOR SECURITY HERE, PRODIGY...

...GUN IT!

ALERT. REDUCE SPEED AND PRESENT IDENTIFICATION.

TZZAKK

ZAKK

ZAKK

NONCOMPLIANCE. COUNTERMEASURES DEPLOYED.

WAH-HOOOO!

IT TICKLES!

KRIZZZ

Shortly...

WE BROKE OUT OF CAMP JUST TO DRINK BEER ON THE BEACH?

WELL, WITH BAT-BOY LOOKING LIKE HE DOES, AND PRODIGY ALL OVER THE TV, OUR OPTIONS ARE LIMITED. BUT HEY, WE'RE FREE!

AWW...I'M OLD ENOUGH TO DIE FOR MY COUNTRY BUT NOT DRINK A BEER?

SORRY, KID. YOU'RE UNDERAGE... AND BY THE WAY, YOU'RE DRIVING.

Y'KNOW... WE COULD ALWAYS GO SKINNY-DIPPING.

SERIOUSLY?

ALL RIGHT.

YOU BET. OFF WITH 'EM, MISTER.

OBOY OBOY OBOY...

HEY!

I ASSURE YOU, I'M COMPLETELY NAKED.

BUT I MIGHT CHANGE BACK TO HUMAN FORM ONCE I'M IN THE WATER...IF *ANNEX* COMES IN.

REALLY?

AH, WHAT THE HELL... CANNONBALL!

NOT GOING IN?

I, UH, CAN'T SWIM.

CAN'T DROWN, EITHER.

I THINK I'LL JUST STAY HERE.

NOT A DRINKING MAN?

BEER DOESN'T AFFECT ME. I CAN'T GET DRUNK. CAN'T REALLY FEEL *ANYTHING*...WELL, I CAN TASTE. BUT I LIKE POP BETTER THAN BEER.

CAN'T FEEL ANYTHING, HUH? THAT MEAN YOU CAN'T GET BURNED?

UH, NO.

INTERESTING. SEE, MY BODY'S ALWAYS RED-HOT. A SIDE EFFECT OF MY ABILITIES.

I CAN'T GET CLOSE TO OTHER PEOPLE WITHOUT SEVERELY BURNING THEM. YOU'RE THE FIRST GUY I'VE MET SINCE I GOT MY POWERS THAT I COULD ACTUALLY TOUCH...

...ACTUALLY KISS...

Y-YOU'RE REAL PRETTY... BUT, UH, WHEN I SAID I CAN'T FEEL ANYTHING...

SHH... FOR ONCE IN YOUR LIFE, BUTTERBALL, SHUT UP FOR A MINUTE.

DON'T TALK. DON'T MOVE. JUST... LIE THERE...

HEY, EMERY'S TAKING OFF WITH THE JEEP!

GUESS I'M NOT DRIVING. CAN I HAVE A BEER NOW?

FORGET THE BEER, BATWING. WE'VE GOT TO CATCH UP TO HIM.

I GOTTA GO.

AW, NO... THE BRASS CAME LOOKING FOR US.

WHAT'D YOU THINK-- BREAKING OUT WOULDN'T ATTRACT ATTENTION?

I WAS KINDA MORE FOCUSED ON GETTING OUT THAN WHAT CAME AFTER.

QUIET, GUYS. I CAN ALMOST HEAR WHAT EMERY'S SAYING.

WHY'D YOU DO IT, EMERY?

I WAS HUNGRY. Y'ALL AIN'T BEEN LETTING ME EAT ANYTHING BUT VEGETABLES AND TOFU, AND I JUST COULDN'T TAKE IT NO MORE.

CONSTRICTOR SAW YOU RIDING ON THE HOOD OF THE JEEP. YOU DIDN'T DO THIS ALONE.

I HELD DOWN THE GAS PEDAL WITH A CINDERBLOCK, SIR. IT WAS JUST ME.

WOW. DO I FEEL LIKE A JACKASS.

YEAH, THE KID MANNED UP, BUT IT WON'T MEAN SQUAT IF WE'RE NOT BACK AT THE BARRACKS FOR BED CHECK, SO LET'S--

BA-WHOOOM

AH...HOW CONVENIENT.

OUR TARGET LEFT THE BASE TO MEET US. ISN'T THAT CONSIDERATE, MR. HYDE?

VERY CIVILIZED OF HIM, COBRA.

THAT'S KING COBRA, IDIOT!

HEY, MAULER--A C-NOTE SAYS THESE TWO CAN'T WASTE THE TASKMASTER WITHOUT TRYIN' TO KILL EACH OTHER FIRST.

NO BET, FIREBRAND.

NOW LET'S GET 'EM!

WHOA.

BRING IT ON, LOSERS!

DON'T WORRY, SIR, WE'VE GOT YOUR BACK!

ANNEX, NO!

YOU'RE NOWHERE NEAR READY FOR--

--THIS.

BTAMM

OH GOD.

THANK YOU, MY DEAR. THOSE FLAMES DIDN'T HURT, BUT THEY MADE ME RED-HOT... AS YELLOWJACKET CAN ATTEST!

GGGGG

NGAHH!

GET... GHH...

KRAMM ...OFF!

HYDE! COBRA, HE'S DOWN!

DAMN IT, WE'RE TOO HEAVILY OUTNUMBERED. THEY'LL HAVE BACKUP HERE SOON--WE HAVEN'T GOT TIME FOR THIS NONSENSE. MAULER-- THE FAT ONE!

ALL RIGHT-- EVERYONE STAND DOWN OR I BLAST THE FAT KID'S HEAD OFF.

FIREBRAND, KILL TASKMASTER. ANYONE ELSE MOVES, AND THE KID DIES.

DID YOU HEAR ME? DROP YOUR WEAPONS OR--

SHZAKKKK

OUCH.

HOLY--!

THE YOUTH IS INVULNERABLE!

RETREAT! FOLLOW THE ESCAPE PLAN!

I'LL GO AFTER THEM.

HE CAN'T CATCH THEM ALL. I'LL HELP--

NO. STAMFORD IS THE *LAST* PLACE WE NEED UNTRAINED SUPERHUMANS CHASING DOWN VILLAINS.

THE S.H.I.E.L.D. CAPEKILLERS WILL BE HERE SOON; THEY'LL TAKE UP THE HUNT.

BUT I HAVE TO SAY, TEAM...

...YOU IMPRESSED ME TONIGHT.

WAY TO GO, BIG BUDDY...YOU'RE A HERO!

ME? WOW.

The Next Morning.

WELL, WE'VE MADE UP OUR MIND, EMERY...

...WE'RE SENDING YOU HOME.

IT'S NOT. WE JUST FEEL IT'S WHAT'S BEST. FOR US AND FOR YOU.

BUT...IF THIS IS ABOUT LEAVING CAMP--

BUT THE FIGHT... I THOUGHT I...

NO OFFENSE, BUT IT WAS PLAIN YOU WERE LOST OUT THERE. WE JUST GOT LUCKY THAT THE MAULER CHOSE YOU AS HIS HOSTAGE.

NO REFLECTION ON YOU, SON. SOME PEOPLE HAVE THE MINDSET FOR MILITARY SERVICE, FOR COMBAT... AND SOME DON'T.

YOU HAVE A BRIGHT FUTURE IN SEARCH-AND-RESCUE, HOSTILE ENVIRONMENT EXPLORATION, ANY NUMBER OF FIELDS. JUST NOT WITH THE INITIATIVE.

DON'T WORRY-- YOU'LL BE GIVEN I.D. STATING YOU'RE IN FULL COMPLIANCE WITH THE REGISTRATION ACT.

YOU GET TO GO HOME. GET ON WITH YOUR LIFE. CONGRATULATIONS, SON.

LUCKY SON OF A--

FOR REAL. I WISH I WAS GOING HOME.

ME TOO. EMAIL US ABOUT WHAT'S GOING ON IN THE REAL WORLD, WILLYA, PAL?

THEY DON'T GET IT. NONE OF 'EM.

I GOT BEAT BY THE NEW WARRIORS ONCE. YOU?

HAWKEYE AND ANT-MAN. TELL ANYONE AND I'LL KILL YOU.

LIKEWISE. OKAY...LET'S DO THIS.

HEY, KID. BEFORE YOU GO, WE GOT UNFINISHED BUSINESS.

The End